Welcome to the Grove

When you step into a redwood grove, you'll feel it right away. The air is cooler. Everything is still and quiet. It's a peaceful, open place, where just a few kinds of plants grow on the forest floor.

This book introduces you to every plant you're likely to find there.

We'll start with an easy-to-use Flower Blossom Finder, organized by color. After that, you'll find a Berry Finder and a Tree Leaf Finder.

You'll likely find your plant's name in the first few pages, but I hope you don't stop there. If you find only the name, you might forget it by tomorrow.

Think of the **Finders** as a doorway into the rest of the book. Once you know a plant's name, turn to its **Plant Page**. There you'll find illustrated plant stories that will help you remember it. You'll also find pages on ferns and shrubs not included in the Finders.

The more you explore, the more familiar these plants will become. Over time, you'll spot them in different seasons and places. Before long, you'll know them well, like an old friend.

And soon, you'll find yourself stopping to look – no longer just passing through the woods.

Adder's Tongue

Trillium

Red Clintonia

Huckleberry

Toyon

Redwood Sorrel

Redwood Violet

Sword Fern

A Forest From the Age of Giants

Coast redwoods have been around since the time of the dinosaurs. In that age of giants, size was often an advantage. It certainly worked out that way for the giant redwoods who were able to shade out potential competitors.

To this day, most weeds can't survive in the grove.

California native plants, on the other hand, have had millions of years to adapt. They've evolved to thrive in the cool, shady, damp, and slightly acidic soil beneath the redwoods. The plants you'll find in the grove have been neighbors for eons.

Let's take a look…

Table of Contents

Finders
    Blossom Finder   3
    Berry Finder   6
    Tree Leaf Finder   7

Illustrated Plant Stories
    Wildflowers   8
    Trees   26
    Shrubs   36
    Ferns   46

Final Thoughts   47

Acknowledgements   48

Copyright © 2025 by PlantID.net

Blossom Finder – Pale Pink to Yellow

Find your flower. Turn to its page for pictures and stories.

Pacific Starflower
1"; 5 to 9 pointed petals. [p. 9]

Wood Rose
1"; 5 floppy petals. [p.37]

Huckleberry
¼" hanging urns. [p. 38]

Red Clintonia
2" cluster; 6 petals. [p. 10]

Columbine
¾"; Hanging, fancy. [p. 11]

Monkey Flower
1"; Many trumpet flowers. [p. 39]

Leopard Lily
3"; upside-down lily. [p. 12]

Redwood Violet
1"; yellow violet. [p. 13]

Bay Laurel (tree)
½"; 6 petals, clusters. [p. 30]

Finders 3

Blossom Finder – Whites

Find your flower. Turn to its page for pictures and stories.

Redwood Sorrel
½"; 5 white/pink petals. [p. 14]

Milkmaids
¾"; 4 separate petals. [p. 15]

Miner's Lettuce
¼"; circular leaf. [p. 16]

Wild Cucumber
½"; 5 narrow petals. [p. 17]

Thimbleberry
1½"; 5 pointed petals. [p. 40]

Pacific Trillium
2"; 3 petals over 3 leaves. [p. 18]

Red Elderberry
3" dense cluster of tiny flowers. [p. 41]

Toyon
Branched cluster. [p. 42]

Madrone
¼" urns hanging on stem. [p. 35]

Blossom Finder – Whites to Purple

Find your flower. Turn to its page for pictures and stories.

Fairy Bells
½"; under leaves.
[p. 19]

Slim Solomon
¼"; Open cluster.
[p. 20]

Fat Solomon
¼"; Tight column.
[p. 21]

CA Buckeye
6" cylinder of fluffy flowers. [p. 34]

Elk Clover
1" spheres of tiny flowers. [p. 44]

Cow Parsnip
6" flat array on stalks. [p. 22]

Coltsfoot
½" tight clusters on stalks. [p. 23]

Adder's Tongue
¾"; flower in 3s.
[p. 24]

Wild Ginger
¾"; 3 maroon petals.
[p. 25]

Berry Finder

Huckleberry
Dark, hanging [38]

Elk Clover
Waxy, erect [44]

Red Clintonia
Shiny, umbrella [10]

Slim Solomon
Loose bunch [20]

Fat Solomon
Tight bunch [21]

Red Elderberry
Branched stalks [41]

Fairy Bells
Few hanging [19]

Madrone
Orange to red [35]

Toyon
Shiny, hanging [42]

Wood Rose
Rose hip [37]

Thimbleberry
Like raspberry [40]

Tree Leaf Finder

Find your leaf. Turn to its page for pictures and stories.

Coast Redwood
Short needles, flat bunches. [p. 27]

Douglas Fir
Short needles, all directions. [p. 28]

Tanbark Oak
Leathery, parallel veins, fuzzy back. [p. 29]

Bay Laurel
Narrow, dark, waxy, strong smell. [p. 30]

Arroyo Willow
Narrow, pale underneath. [p. 31]

Red Alder
Wavy margins, pale underneath. [p. 32]

Big-Leaf Maple
Big maple-leaf shape. [p. 33]

CA Buckeye
Leaflets form a palm shape. [p. 34]

Madrone
Leaves connect separately to the branch. [p. 35]

Finders 7

Wildflowers in the Grove

Here are the wildflowers you'll encounter in the grove. Their flowers create color accents that attract pollinators.

If your flower has woody stems, you'll find it in the shrub section starting on page 36.

Milkmaids   **Redwood Sorrel**

Redwood Violet

Pacific Starflower (*Lysimachia latifolia*)

Blooms from April to July. It's under 1 foot tall.

Pacific Starflower grows close to the ground in damp, shady places.

It's a delicate woodland flower, less than an inch across, with more or less 7 pointed petals. The actual petal count can vary – this species has some wiggle room in its flower design.

Photo by Steve Matson

The leaves and flowers all grow from a single spot at the top of the stem. The leaves are often different sizes, which catches my eye.

Photo by Steve Matson

Painting © John Muir Laws

Red Clintonia *(Clintonia andrewsiana)*

Blooms from April to July. It's about 1 foot tall.

Clintonia's tight sphere of reddish-pink lily flowers stands out dramatically in the grove.

The flower cluster floats high above a bed of wide, parallel-veined leaves that radiate out in a circle. The leaves are big, to gather in as much light as possible. Using photosynthesis, the leaves convert light and water into food needed to create its dramatic floral display.

Shiny blue berries, full of seeds, replace the flowers. They remind me of shiny beads. Although poisonous to humans, deer eat them and distribute the seeds.

Photo by Keir Morse

Photo by Keir Morse

Photo by Zoya Akulova-Barlow

Columbine *(Aquilegia formosa)*

Blooms from March to May. It's 1 or 2 feet tall.

Red Columbine flowers hang upside down from a drooping stem. Once a flower is pollinated though, the stem straightens and seed pods stand erect while they mature.

Photo by Wilde Legard   Photo by Keir Morse

Small leaflets, in 3s, remind me of tiny mittens.

Erect flower stalks can rise several feet in the air.

Painting © John Muir Laws   Photo by Julie Kierstead Nelson

Wildflowers   11

Leopard Lily (*Lilium pardalinum*)

Blooms from June to July. It grows 3 to 7 feet tall.

Here is a flower like no other in the grove. Elaborate orange and yellow lily flowers hang down from tall stalks, often in colonies of several plants. They like to keep their feet wet, growing in marshes or next to streams. Narrow, pointed leaves form whorls along the stem.

Painting © John Muir Laws

Photo © Neal Kramer

Like a leopard, the flowers have dark spots on a lighter background. They catch the attention of swallowtail butterflies, native bees and hummingbirds which have no problem approaching the flower from below. These favored visitors receive nice drinks of nectar while they accidentally move pollen from one flower to the next.

Photo by Steve Matson

Redwood Violet (*Viola sempervirens*)

Blooms from January to May. It grows low to the ground.

This beautiful yellow violet is marked with striking maroon lines that guide the way to its nectar glands. Because maroon is the complementary color to yellow, these nectar guides stand out, attracting bees and butterflies.

Violet leaves are heart shaped and leathery, often showing purple spots.

Drawing © John Muir Laws

Photo by Steve Matson

Photo by John Doyen

Wildflowers

Redwood Sorrel (Oxalis oregana)

Blooms from February to June. It grows low to the ground.

Redwood Sorrel is the most common wildflower found among the needles of the redwood grove. It thrives in the grove's damp, acidic soil but outside coastal evergreen forests, it's rarely found.

Photo by Steve Matson

½ inch flowers have 5 delicately striped petals with rounded tips.

Photo by Wilde Legard

Heart-shaped leaflets grow in threes. They taste sour.

Redwood Sorrel creates a soft green carpet on the forest floor. Its pale flowers, ranging from white to pink, stand out in the deep shade.

Delicate, clover-shaped leaves open wide to catch the dim light. But when a direct sunbeam breaks through or when night falls, they protect themselves by folding up like tiny umbrellas.

Painting © John Muir Laws

Milkmaids (Cardamine californica)

Blooms from January to May. It grows about 1 foot tall.

Milkmaids are one of the first bloomers in the redwood grove. I love seeing their bright white blossoms because I know it's the beginning of flower season.

Bright white flowers are about ½ inch across. They form a loose cluster at the top of the stem.

Photo by Steve Matson

4 petals lie flat, making a shape like a windmill with rounded tips. If your plant has 5 petals, check out Redwood Sorrel or Miner's Lettuce.

Photo by Steve Matson

Drawing © John Muir Laws

Leaves near the bottom of the plant are shaped like a stool for a milkmaid to sit on. Leaves higher up the stem are deeply cut and pointy.

Wildflowers 15

Miner's Lettuce (*Claytonia perfoliata*)

Blooms from February to May. It grows close to the ground.

Miner's lettuce forms carpets of green, growing in damp, shady places.

It features a round top leaf that surrounds the stem, with one or a few tiny (1/8 inch) white flowers clustered on top.

Photo by William Follette

The leaves below the top circular leaf are different. They're diamond-shaped, at the end of stalks. They taste like lettuce, just as the name suggests.

Drawing © John Muir Laws

Photo by Wilde Legard

Wild Cucumber (*Marah fabacea*)

Blooms from February to April.

This fast-growing vine climbs other plants by grabbing them with stalks that twist around anything they touch. Their coiling pulls the rest of the plant up.

The leaves are big (2 to 5 inches) and make me think of mittens.

Photo by Steve Matson

Photo by Wilde Legard

Flowers grow spiky fruits, about 2 inches across. They remind me of a miniature watermelon, with prickles. Fruits explode when ripe, propelling their large seeds away from the mother plant.

The bumps on the pickles we eat are remnants of the spines from their wild cucumber ancestors.

Photo by Keir Morse

Photo by Steve Matson

Wildflowers 17

Pacific Trillium (*Trillium ovatum*)

Blooms from February to May. It's a low growing flower of great beauty.

I love to find this graceful circle of threes on the forest floor.

You'll find many young Trilliums without a bloom. They gather energy for several years before blooming.

Photo by Wendy Wilmes

After pollination, the white petals fade to a maroon shade, letting bees know it has no more pollen for them.

Line drawing © Kristin Jakob

Photo by William Follette

Fairy Bells (*Prosartes hookeri*)

Blooms from March to June. It grows to about 2 feet tall.

You can find Fairy Bells by the side of the trail, in shady, damp areas.

Leaves are wide and face up. Underneath the leaves, if you look carefully, you can find delicate, lily-like flowers, ½ inch across.

Photo by Barry Breckling

Photo by Wilde Legard

In the fall, shiny red berries peek out from under the leaves. They're a good food source for ground-feeding birds and slugs.

Photo by William Follette

Slim Solomon (*Maianthemum stellatum*)

Blooms from May to June. It grows to about 2 feet tall.

The first thing I notice is the beautiful, broad, smooth-edged leaves lying flat and open to pick up the sunlight. A few small, spaced-apart flowers decorate the top of the stem.

Photo by William Follette

The Latin *stellatum* means "stars". The tiny flowers sparkle like a constellation in the night sky. As the flowers fade, widely spaced berries take their place – starting green, then turning red, and eventually black.

Photo by Wilde Legard

Photo by Keir Morse

Fat Solomon (*Maianthemum racemosum*)

Blooms from May to July. It grows to about 2 feet tall.

Fat Solomon is very similar to Slim Solomon but has broader leaves and a tighter cluster of flowers.

Photo by Barry Breckling

A column of tiny white flowers decorates the top of the stem. The flowers transform into tightly bunched green berries that turn red when they mature.

Photo by Keir Morse

Photo by Bruce Homer-Smith

Cow Parsnip (*Heracleum maximum*)

Blooms from June to July. It can grow 6 feet tall and more, very tall for a flower without a woody stem.

This is the umbrella plant. Its round flower clusters are held on stalks that radiate like the spokes of an umbrella, and the tiny flowers in each cluster sit on their own umbrella-like stems.

The umbrella structure is common in the Carrot Family, which includes Queen Anne's Lace, Poison Hemlock and Angelica.

Painting © John Muir Laws

Photo by Susan Mayne

Painting © John Muir Laws

Leaves are huge, up to a foot across! Stems are thick, ribbed and hollow, a good structure to support this tall plant.

Photo © Neal Kramer

Coltsfoot (*Petasites frigidus*)

Blooms from March to May. It grows to 2 feet tall.

Coltsfoot grows in wet, shady areas. It has a thick vertical stem ending in a cluster of flower heads. Each head holds its flowers in a tight bunch.

Photo by Steve Matson

Photo by Steve Matson

Flies and bees like pollinating these concentrated flower clusters.

Although small leaves grow on the stem, a big round leaf grows directly from the root

The bottom leaf is distinctive – often 6 inches across, round with deep indents, and fuzzy on the bottom. It reminds some people of a colt's hoof print, thus its common name.

This big leaf also gives the plant its scientific name. *Petasites* is derived from a Greek word for a broad-brimmed hat.

Photo by Steve Matson

Fetid Adder's Tongue (Scoliopus bigelovii)

Blooms from January to March. It grows about a foot tall.

This early bloomer is tricky to find but exciting when you do.

You'll probably notice the spotted leaves first. They're long and wide with a random pattern of big brown spots. Like other lilies, the leaves have parallel veins and end in a point.

The brown-striped lily flower is less obvious. Its narrow petals and subtle brown stripes blend into the dark forest floor. But if you find it, look closely – its perfect symmetry and quiet elegance make it one of the forest's hidden gems. It's one of my favorites.

This flower isn't pollinated by the usual assortment of bees and butterflies that use visual cues to find the flower. Instead, it's pollinated by fungus gnats – tiny insects that hover low over the forest floor.

Fetid Adder's Tongue gives off a musky scent that mimics decaying plant material and fungus – just what the gnats like to eat. As they move from flower to flower, the gnats carry pollen with them.

Ground insects distribute this plant's seeds too. Fetid Adder's Tongue seeds have a fatty coating that ants love to eat. The ants carry the seeds back to their nests, eat the coating, and leave the rest untouched, nicely spreading them for growing next season.

Photo by William Follette

Photo by Neal Kramer

Photo by Zoya Akulova-Barlow

Wild Ginger (Asarum caudatum)

Blooms from March to May – grows low to the ground.

Look for a carpet of 4-inch heart-shaped leaves along the side of a moist, shady path.

Then look underneath to find surprising maroon flowers. They form a cup topped by three triangular structures that end in a thready tail. *Caudatum* is Latin for "tailed."

Growing close to the ground, these flowers are pollinated by beetles, flies and gnats. As with Fetid Adder's Tongue, their seeds are distributed by soil-dwelling insects who are drawn to their oily coverings.

Painting © John Muir Laws

Photo by Keir Morse

Photo by Keir Morse

Rub the leaves and you'll smell ginger – though not the ginger we use in cooking.

Roots grow horizontally underground, holding food and water. They grow new shoots from time to time, creating a cloned colony of Wild Gingers.

Wildflowers

Trees in the Grove

Here are the trees in the grove. Look for their beautiful seed containers.

Redwood **Douglas Fir**

Big Leaf Maple **Bay Laurel** **Madrone**

Coast Redwood (*Sequoia sempervirens*)

Coast Redwoods cast cool, deep shade. Their needles acidify the soil. They set the living conditions for everything underneath.

Coast Redwoods often grow 500 to 2,000 years. Over those centuries, they survive dozens of fires, floods and insect invasions. And, steadily growing bigger, they become kings of the forest, frequently reaching over 200 feet tall.

Photo © Neal Kramer

Redwoods are columnar giants. Their roots are shallow but interlock, providing a stable foundation.

Photo by Wilde Legard

The bark is reddish, soft and fibrous.

Photo by Susan Mayne

Needles lie flat.

Trees   27

Douglas Fir (*Pseudotsuga menziesii*)

Douglas Fir and Coast Redwood are the only conifers you're likely to notice in the grove. They're easy to tell apart.

Redwood needles lie in a flat plane while Douglas Fir needles point in all directions.

Redwood bark is reddish, soft and fibrous. Douglas Fir bark is dark, hard, and deeply furrowed.

Photo by Bruce Homer-Smith

Painting © John Muir Laws

Short needles point in all directions.

Painting © John Muir Laws

Cones have "mouse tails" hanging between the scales.

Both Douglas Fir and Coast Redwood thrive in the fog. However, Douglas Firs need less water than redwoods, so they often become the primary tree on slopes above redwood groves.

Firs and redwoods share a complex ecosystem in their tops. Mosses, lichens and even salamanders live high up in their branches.

Tanbark Oak (*Notholithocarpus densiflorus*)

Tanbark Oaks are easy to recognize. They have leathery leaves with lots of veins. The back of the leaf is pale and often fuzzy.

These trees are common in the understory but they usually grow shorter than the towering trees around them. Many old-growth giants were logged in the 1800s for their leather-curing tannins. Today, they face a new challenge: sudden oak death.

In the spring, if you look for them, you can find pollen spikes that rise up from the leaves, sending millions of bits of pollen in the air.

Photos by Keir Morse

Tanbark Oak acorns have "bad hair" – hundreds of short, curlicue spikes on the acorn cap.

Photo by Zoya Akulova-Barlow

Photo by William Follette

California Bay Laurel (Umbellularia californica)

California Bay Laurel adds a spicy smell to the quiet, moist air of the redwood grove. Rub a leaf and smell your fingers. The aroma is quite similar to the bay leaves in your kitchen.

Although they can grow to 100 feet in open places, Bay Laurels are understory trees in the grove.

Painting © John Muir Laws

Photo by Zoya Akulova-Barlow

Leaves are dark green and shiny. They're long, narrow, pointed and smooth-edged.

A ring of daughter trees can grow around the original, making a very wide base.

Photo by Julie Kierstead Nelson

Photo © Neal Kramer

Small clusters of yellowish flowers grow at the base of the leaves in the spring.

Pollinated flowers turn into a small, ½ inch avocado-like fruits.

Arroyo Willow (*Salix lasiolepis*)

You'll find Arroyo Willows and Red Alders next to streams where they can keep their feet wet. They lean over the water to find light.

They offer nice cover for birds – listen for their calls and songs.

Fuzzy hairs cover both male and female catkins, protecting the tiny, delicate flowers.

Painting © John Muir Laws

Leaves are distinctive: long, bulging near the tip, smooth sided, and pale on the bottom.

Photo by Wild Legard

Photo by William Follette

Male catkins distribute thousands of pollen grains in the air.

Photo by Wilde Legard

Female catkins, on separate trees, create fuzzy seeds that fly off on the wind.

Trees 31

Red Alder *(Alnus rubra)*

You'll often find Red Alders near Arroyo Willows along the stream.

Alder leaves are soft, with many indented veins and a saw-toothed leaf margin.

In spring, male catkins hang from the branches, releasing reddish pollen into the air. Nearby, on the same tree, tiny female flowers sit inside small, cone-like structures where they catch the airborne pollen. They form seeds, tucked safely inside their little wooden caves.

Photo by Zoya Akulova-Barlow

Photos © Neal Kramer

Photo by Bruce Homer-Smith

Once its leaves drop, Red Alder's white bark stands out against the darker forest.

Big Leaf Maple (Acer macrophyllum)

Where a tree falls down in the grove, Big Leaf Maple saplings grow quickly into the light. You'll recognize this tree easily based on its big maple leaf.

Paintings © John Muir Laws

Photo by Wilde Legard

Photo by Wilde Legard

Photo by Daniel Passarini

In spring, look for the beautiful hanging flowers. They offer a sumptuous feast for bees and other flying insects. And in the fall, yellow leaves glow in the light, casting a warm color across the forest.

Trees 33

California Buckeye (Aesculus californica)

Like the maple, California Buckeye reaches for light in places where grove trees have fallen.

Painting © John Muir Laws   Photo © Neal Kramer

Buckeyes start their seasonal pattern early. 5-fingered green leaves bud in late winter. Flowers are in full bloom by spring. By late summer, the leaves have fallen and large leather-covered buckeyes appear. Up to 2 inches, they're the largest seed of any native plant.

Photo by Toni Corelli

Columns of sweet-smelling flowers provide a feast for native bees and butterflies. European bees find the flowers' pollen toxic.

Madrone (*Arbutus menziesii*)

Unlike most trees, the first thing you'll notice about Madrone is its lovely bark. An outer layer of loose, small squares often peels off to show smooth shades of brown, tan and green. Touch it, and the silky surface feels surprisingly cool.

Thousands of delicate Madrone flowers and berries grow on mature trees. The berries persist on the tree well into winter, providing welcome food for animals.

Photo by William Follette

Painting © John Muir Laws

Photo © Neal Kramer

Photo © Neal Kramer

Photo by Toni Corelli

You might notice similar bark on Manzanitas. The difference is easy to spot: Manzanitas are shrubs, and their bark is a deeper red.

Trees 35

Shrubs in the Grove

Shrubs have many woody stems. In the grove, a surprising number have big flowers and berries.

Toyon

Sticky Monkey Flower

Wood Rose

Wood Rose *(Rosa gymnocarpa)*

Blooms from May to June. This shrub typically grows 5 feet tall.

Wood roses form a loose layer of leaves and flowers at its outer edge, giving an airy look. It is found in shady places from California to British Columbia.

Pink rose flowers, about 1 inch across, grow singly or in small clusters throughout the shrub

Petals are floppy, surrounding a tangle of yellow-tipped stamens.

Photo by Keir Morse

Leaflets form the ladder-shape typical of roses, with many leaflet pairs on slender stalks.

Painting © John Muir Laws

Prickles are densely grouped, slender and straight. Other roses have thicker, more-widely-spaced prickles.

Also, other roses have leafy growths at the base of their rosehip, but our rosehip is bare.

Photo © Neal Kramer

Shrubs

Huckleberry *(Vaccinium ovatum)*

Blooms from May to June. This shrub typically grows 4 feet tall.

I love finding huckleberry bushes, with their thick, saw-toothed leaves. They often have drops of water on their waxy surface. Stems and leaves frequently show red.

Photos by Zoya Akulova-Barlow

Photo © Neal Kramer

Flowers are tiny, upside-down urns, similar to other members of the Heath Family, such as Madrone and Manzanita. Dark huckleberry fruits come out in late summer, a favorite of many animals.

Photo by Wilde Legard

Photo by Wilde Legard

Sticky Monkey Flower (Diplacus aurantiacus)

Blooms from March to August. This shrub typically grows 4 feet tall.

Sticky Monkey Flower is an easy plant to learn – look for lots of orange flowers and sticky, dark green leaves.

Photo by William Follette

The leaves are distinctive: they join the stem in pairs (opposite leaves). They're narrow, thick, and have indented veins. The leaf edges curl under.

Bees and hummingbirds pollinate the bright orange flowers.

Stickiness on the leaves helps pollen stick to the pollinators. It also deters herbivores and insects from stealing the rich nectar at the base of the trumpet flowers.

Painting © John Muir Laws

Thimbleberry *(Rubus parviflorus)*

Blooms from March to May. This shrub typically grows 6 feet tall.

You'll find Thimbleberry growing in moist, shady places.

Thimbleberries are members of the Rose Family, like the Wood Rose a few pages back. White 2-inch flowers have 5 floppy petals and a golden crown of stamens in the middle.

The leaves remind me of fuzzy maple leaves, thick and soft, showing indented veins. They're big, up to 10 inches across, and often cover the outside surface of the shrub.

Photo by Wilde Legard

Thimbleberry has narrow, many-branched, woody stems, sort of like blackberries. However, Thimbleberry stems have no prickles. Thimbleberry thickets provide cover for lots of birds and small mammals.

Painting © John Muir Laws   Painting © John Muir Laws

Thimbleberry berries remind me of raspberries, but they're softer and fall apart more easily. Like a thimble, they're bumpy on the outside and hollow on the inside.

Red Elderberry *(Sambucus racemosa)*

Blooms from April to July. This shrub typically grows 10 feet tall.

Other elderberries grow in dry places but you'll often find this big one near water. Its extensive roots help stabilize soil in the grove during floods, a benefit to the giant redwoods it lives beneath.

Photo © Steve Matson

3-inch clusters of fragrant white flowers, full of nectar, attract a wide variety of pollinators, including bees, flies and beetles. Plentiful red berries feed lots of birds and mammals in the fall.

Painting © John Muir Laws

Photo © Neal Kramer

Large leaflets have serrated edges and connect to a central stalk.

Sambucus means "musical instrument". You can hollow out a dry branch to create a flute but be careful – its sap is poisonous.

Toyon *(Heteromeles arbutifolia)*

Blooms from June to August. This shrub typically grows 10 feet tall.

Toyon grows dense clusters of miniature (¼ inch) rose flowers. A wide variety of bees and butterflies visit them to sip their nectar. Toyon needs a lot of visiting, with up to 100 flowers per cluster and dozens of clusters per plant. At night, beetles crawl among the fragrant flowers and continue pollination.

Each pollinated flower turns into a red berry, providing a bonanza of food for birds and mammals throughout the winter. Toyon is sometimes called Christmas Berry because the berries ripen in early December and stay on their stalks until they're eaten, well into the new year.

Photo by Wilde Legard

Photo by Julie Kierstead Nelson

Each 3-inch leaf is stiff, grows on its own stalk and has serrated edges. Similarly shaped Bay Laurel leaves have smooth edges.

Photo by Zoya Akulova-Barlow

Toyon is widespread in coastal California and the Sierras, doing well in the cool of the grove but also in dryer, sunny places.

California Hazelnut (Corylus cornuta)

Blooms from January to March. This shrub is typically 8 feet tall.

The first thing you'll notice about this shrub is its super-soft leaves and red-and-yellow spotted catkins. The leaves are fuzzy, have indented veins and toothed edges.

Catkins hang down from leaf joints, growing red and yellow pollen grains until they're dry enough to drift away on the wind.

Fuzzy leaves

Photo by Steve Matson

Male catkin full of pollen

Photo by Steve Matson

Female flower

Photo © Neal Kramer

Female flowers have small protrusions that pick up airborne pollen. They grow into hazelnuts.

Hazelnut

Photo by Wilde Legard

Hazel sends up straight shoots which were traditionally used by the Miwok people to make arrows.

Shrubs 43

Elk Clover *(Aralia californica)*

Blooms from June to September. This shrub is typically 8 feet tall.

This is no clover. You'll find it growing enthusiastically, often right out of a streambed, taller than you.

Photo by Steve Matson

Photo by Keir Morse

Photo © Neal Kramer

You'll notice these plants because they fill up space in the airy floor of the redwood grove. Elk Clover creates a canopy of hundreds of large leaflets, each up to a foot long!

Spheres of tiny white flowers grow on thick stalks above the leaves. They turn into smooth, dark berries in the fall, providing food for birds and mammals.

Elk Clover is technically not a shrub because its stems are not woody. But it's big like a shrub, so I've placed it here.

Poison Oak *(Toxicodendron diversilobum)*

Blooms from March to June. This shrub grows as a bush and also as a vine. I've heard that it's the most common shrub in California.

Poison Oak leaves will probably give you an itchy rash if you brush against them. The rule is, "leaves 3, let it be." Animals don't seem to be affected by these toxic oils.

Painting © John Muir Laws

Photo by William Follette

Look for beautiful, tiny Poison Oak flowers and berries.

In fall, red leaves cast a glow in the shady understory.

Photo by Steve Matson

Photo by Toni Corelli

Photo by Keir Morse

Shrubs 45

Ferns in the Grove

Ferns do well in the damp, shady, acidic soil of the grove. Here are four types you're likely to notice.

Western Sword Ferns grow several feet tall. Leaflets have a "thumb" at their base (the hilt of the sword).

Photo by Alf Fengler

Gold Back Ferns form small triangles low to the ground. They often have gold on the back.

Photo by Steve Matson

Maidenhair Ferns are made up of delicate fan-like leaflets with lots of space between.

Painting © John Muir Laws

Giant Horsetails grow 6 or more feet tall with lots of narrow, horizontal branches.

Photo © Neal Kramer

Ferns and Allies   46

Final Thoughts

Taken as a whole, the grove shows some interesting patterns.

Most of the flowers in redwood groves are pale in color. Maybe that helps pollinators find them in the shade under the trees.

Surprisingly, nearly a quarter of the 17 wildflowers in this book are lilies: Red Clintonia, Leopard Lily, Fairy Bells and Fetid Adder's Tongue. Redwood groves are a great place for lilies to grow, with soft light, cool temperatures, moist but well-drained soil, and little competition from plants less suited to this special habitat.

The grove's stable, moist conditions also help almost every shrub grow elaborate berries or nuts. Many animals feast on them and spread the seeds, adding strength to the ecosystem.

Ferns are a familiar sight in the redwood grove. Ferns and redwoods have grown alongside each other for millions of years.

I like to think of grove trees in three groups:

1) **Redwoods and Douglas Firs** stand tall, using their height to get plenty of sunlight to drive their growth.

2) **Madrones, Maples, Tanbark Oak and Buckeye** scatter their seeds on the forest floor and grow quickly in sunny openings when a giant tree falls.

3) **Alders, Bay Laurels and Willows** hug the side of streams, keeping their feet wet. They lean out over the water to get sunlight.

Over eons, hundreds of living species have woven themselves into a rich web of life in the grove. Birds, mammals, slugs, newts, salamanders, frogs, lizards, snakes and hosts of insects visit the plants on many errands. Lichens, mosses and mushrooms cling to trunks. Fungus networks and microorganisms exchange minerals and water with plant roots.

Most of this complexity is hidden from us as we walk through the grove. But if we slow down and really look, we can begin to notice small pieces of it. The redwood grove is a living whole, ancient, precious and intricate beyond our understanding.

Acknowledgements

This book is a production of **PlantID.net**, a collaboration of volunteers who love learning about and describing California's wild plants. Visit the site to explore local plant guides and richly illustrated plant stories. Here's the guide for plants in the redwood grove:

The idea for this book took shape during COVID, in conversations with **Mia Monroe**, a longtime ranger and educator at Muir Woods. We imagined a visitor-friendly introduction to the plant community beneath the coast redwoods. She and **Elliot Gunnison**, Muir Woods ecologist, helped me assemble the initial list of species.

Kate Wing, a Muir Woods docent, refined that list by focusing on the plants people most often encounter on her redwood grove tours. These are the plants beginners want to learn.

Kristin Jacob, my longtime friend and expert on Marin County plants, offered encouragement and helped me confirm the facts.

John Muir Laws, famous painter, naturalist, and author, supported this project with his paintings and thoughtful advice.

I used **ChatGPT** to make wording suggestions to keep my text clear and consistent.

Virginia and **Charlie**, my 3rd and 6th grade grandchildren, showed me where I could make this book simpler and more fun.

Thanks to **M. Raven Brown** for her cover design, featuring **Wendy Wilmes**' glorious Trillium photo.

This book relies heavily on the photographs, drawings, illustrations and paintings donated to **PlantID.net**. This is a non-commercial project. None of us receive compensation from its sales.

AF	Alf Fengler	KM	Keir Morse
BB	Barry Breckling	SGM	Susan Mayne
BHS	Bruce Homer-Smith	SSM	Steve Matson
DP	Daniel Passarini	TC	Toni Corelli
JD	John Doyen	WF	William Follette
JKN	Julie Kierstead Nelson	WL	Wilde Legard
JML	John Muir Laws	WW	Wendy Wilmes
KJ	Kristin Jakob	ZAB	Zoya Akulova-Barlow
NK	Neal Kramer		

Find copyright information at **PlantID.net/Contributors.aspx**.

www.ingramcontent.com/pod-product-compliance
Lightning Source LLC
Chambersburg PA
CBRC101143030426
42337CB00007B/61